Password &
Account Number
Kevin Hwu **Book**

No	Bank	
	Account Number	
	Password	
	Opening date	
	Note	

No	Bank	
	Account Number	
	Password	
	Opening date	
	Note	

No	PC	
	Account Number	
	Password	
	Opening date	
	Note	

No	Bank	
	Account Number	
	Password	
	Opening date	
	Note	

No	Bank	
	Account Number	
	Password	
	Opening date	
	Note	

No	PC	
	Account Number	
	Password	
	Opening date	
	Note	

No	**Bank**	
	Account Number	
	Password	
	Opening date	
	Note	

No	**Bank**	
	Account Number	
	Password	
	Opening date	
	Note	

No	**PC**	
	Account Number	
	Password	
	Opening date	
	Note	

No	Bank	
	Account Number	
	Password	
	Opening date	
	Note	

No	Bank	
	Account Number	
	Password	
	Opening date	
	Note	

No	PC	
	Account Number	
	Password	
	Opening date	
	Note	

No	Bank	
	Account Number	
	Password	
	Opening date	
	Note	

No	Bank	
	Account Number	
	Password	
	Opening date	
	Note	

No	PC	
	Account Number	
	Password	
	Opening date	
	Note	

No	Bank	
	Account Number	
	Password	
	Opening date	
	Note	

No	Bank	
	Account Number	
	Password	
	Opening date	
	Note	

No	PC	
	Account Number	
	Password	
	Opening date	
	Note	

No	Bank	
	Account Number	
	Password	
	Opening date	
	Note	

No	Bank	
	Account Number	
	Password	
	Opening date	
	Note	

No	PC	
	Account Number	
	Password	
	Opening date	
	Note	

No	Bank	
	Account Number	
	Password	
	Opening date	
	Note	

No	Bank	
	Account Number	
	Password	
	Opening date	
	Note	

No	PC	
	Account Number	
	Password	
	Opening date	
	Note	

No	Bank	
	Account Number	
	Password	
	Opening date	
	Note	

No	Bank	
	Account Number	
	Password	
	Opening date	
	Note	

No	PC	
	Account Number	
	Password	
	Opening date	
	Note	

No	Bank	
	Account Number	
	Password	
	Opening date	
	Note	

No	Bank	
	Account Number	
	Password	
	Opening date	
	Note	

No	PC	
	Account Number	
	Password	
	Opening date	
	Note	

No		Bank	
	Account Number		
	Password		
	Opening date		
	Note		

No		Bank	
	Account Number		
	Password		
	Opening date		
	Note		

No		PC	
	Account Number		
	Password		
	Opening date		
	Note		

No	Bank	
	Account Number	
	Password	
	Opening date	
	Note	

No	Bank	
	Account Number	
	Password	
	Opening date	
	Note	

No	PC	
	Account Number	
	Password	
	Opening date	
	Note	

No	Bank	
	Account Number	
	Password	
	Opening date	
	Note	

No	Bank	
	Account Number	
	Password	
	Opening date	
	Note	

No	PC	
	Account Number	
	Password	
	Opening date	
	Note	

No	Bank	
	Account Number	
	Password	
	Opening date	
	Note	

No	Bank	
	Account Number	
	Password	
	Opening date	
	Note	

No	PC	
	Account Number	
	Password	
	Opening date	
	Note	

No	Bank	
	Account Number	
	Password	
	Opening date	
	Note	

No	Bank	
	Account Number	
	Password	
	Opening date	
	Note	

No	PC	
	Account Number	
	Password	
	Opening date	
	Note	

No		Bank	
	Account Number	
	Password	
	Opening date	
	Note	

No		Bank	
	Account Number	
	Password	
	Opening date	
	Note	

No		PC	
	Account Number	
	Password	
	Opening date	
	Note	

No	**Bank**	
	Account Number	
	Password	
	Opening date	
	Note	

No	**Bank**	
	Account Number	
	Password	
	Opening date	
	Note	

No	**PC**	
	Account Number	
	Password	
	Opening date	
	Note	

No	Bank	
	Account Number	
	Password	
	Opening date	
	Note	

No	Bank	
	Account Number	
	Password	
	Opening date	
	Note	

No	PC	
	Account Number	
	Password	
	Opening date	
	Note	

No	Bank	
	Account Number	
	Password	
	Opening date	
	Note	

No	Bank	
	Account Number	
	Password	
	Opening date	
	Note	

No	PC	
	Account Number	
	Password	
	Opening date	
	Note	

No	Bank	
	Account Number	
	Password	
	Opening date	
	Note	

No	Bank	
	Account Number	
	Password	
	Opening date	
	Note	

No	PC	
	Account Number	
	Password	
	Opening date	
	Note	

No	Bank	
	Account Number	
	Password	
	Opening date	
	Note	

No	Bank	
	Account Number	
	Password	
	Opening date	
	Note	

No	PC	
	Account Number	
	Password	
	Opening date	
	Note	

No	Bank	
	Account Number	
	Password	
	Opening date	
	Note	

No	Bank	
	Account Number	
	Password	
	Opening date	
	Note	

No	PC	
	Account Number	
	Password	
	Opening date	
	Note	

No	Bank	
	Account Number	
	Password	
	Opening date	
	Note	

No	Bank	
	Account Number	
	Password	
	Opening date	
	Note	

No	PC	
	Account Number	
	Password	
	Opening date	
	Note	

No	Bank	
	Account Number	
	Password	
	Opening date	
	Note	

No	Bank	
	Account Number	
	Password	
	Opening date	
	Note	

No	PC	
	Account Number	
	Password	
	Opening date	
	Note	

No	Bank	
	Account Number	
	Password	
	Opening date	
	Note	

No	Bank	
	Account Number	
	Password	
	Opening date	
	Note	

No	PC	
	Account Number	
	Password	
	Opening date	
	Note	

No	Bank	
	Account Number	
	Password	
	Opening date	
	Note	

No	Bank	
	Account Number	
	Password	
	Opening date	
	Note	

No	PC	
	Account Number	
	Password	
	Opening date	
	Note	

No	Bank	
	Account Number	
	Password	
	Opening date	
	Note	

No	Bank	
	Account Number	
	Password	
	Opening date	
	Note	

No	PC	
	Account Number	
	Password	
	Opening date	
	Note	

No	Bank	
	Account Number	
	Password	
	Opening date	
	Note	

No	Bank	
	Account Number	
	Password	
	Opening date	
	Note	

No	PC	
	Account Number	
	Password	
	Opening date	
	Note	

No	Bank	
	Account Number	
	Password	
	Opening date	
	Note	

No	Bank	
	Account Number	
	Password	
	Opening date	
	Note	

No	PC	
	Account Number	
	Password	
	Opening date	
	Note	

No	Bank	
	Account Number	
	Password	
	Opening date	
	Note	

No	Bank	
	Account Number	
	Password	
	Opening date	
	Note	

No	PC	
	Account Number	
	Password	
	Opening date	
	Note	

No	Bank	
	Account Number	
	Password	
	Opening date	
	Note	

No	Bank	
	Account Number	
	Password	
	Opening date	
	Note	

No	PC	
	Account Number	
	Password	
	Opening date	
	Note	

No	Bank	
	Account Number	
	Password	
	Opening date	
	Note	

No	Bank	
	Account Number	
	Password	
	Opening date	
	Note	

No	PC	
	Account Number	
	Password	
	Opening date	
	Note	

No	Bank	
	Account Number	
	Password	
	Opening date	
	Note	

No	Bank	
	Account Number	
	Password	
	Opening date	
	Note	

No	PC	
	Account Number	
	Password	
	Opening date	
	Note	

No		Bank	
		Account Number	
		Password	
		Opening date	
		Note	

No		Bank	
		Account Number	
		Password	
		Opening date	
		Note	

No		PC	
		Account Number	
		Password	
		Opening date	
		Note	

No	Bank	
	Account Number	
	Password	
	Opening date	
	Note	

No	Bank	
	Account Number	
	Password	
	Opening date	
	Note	

No	PC	
	Account Number	
	Password	
	Opening date	
	Note	

No	Bank	
	Account Number	
	Password	
	Opening date	
	Note	

No	Bank	
	Account Number	
	Password	
	Opening date	
	Note	

No	PC	
	Account Number	
	Password	
	Opening date	
	Note	

No	Bank	
	Account Number	
	Password	
	Opening date	
	Note	

No	Bank	
	Account Number	
	Password	
	Opening date	
	Note	

No	PC	
	Account Number	
	Password	
	Opening date	
	Note	

No	Bank	
	Account Number	
	Password	
	Opening date	
	Note	

No	Bank	
	Account Number	
	Password	
	Opening date	
	Note	

No	PC	
	Account Number	
	Password	
	Opening date	
	Note	

No	Bank	
	Account Number	
	Password	
	Opening date	
	Note	

No	Bank	
	Account Number	
	Password	
	Opening date	
	Note	

No	PC	
	Account Number	
	Password	
	Opening date	
	Note	

No	Bank	
	Account Number	
	Password	
	Opening date	
	Note	

No	Bank	
	Account Number	
	Password	
	Opening date	
	Note	

No	PC	
	Account Number	
	Password	
	Opening date	
	Note	

No	Bank	
	Account Number	
	Password	
	Opening date	
	Note	

No	Bank	
	Account Number	
	Password	
	Opening date	
	Note	

No	PC	
	Account Number	
	Password	
	Opening date	
	Note	

No	Bank	
	Account Number	
	Password	
	Opening date	
	Note	

No	Bank	
	Account Number	
	Password	
	Opening date	
	Note	

No	PC	
	Account Number	
	Password	
	Opening date	
	Note	

No	Bank	
	Account Number	
	Password	
	Opening date	
	Note	

No	Bank	
	Account Number	
	Password	
	Opening date	
	Note	

No	PC	
	Account Number	
	Password	
	Opening date	
	Note	

No	Bank	
	Account Number	
	Password	
	Opening date	
	Note	

No	Bank	
	Account Number	
	Password	
	Opening date	
	Note	

No	PC	
	Account Number	
	Password	
	Opening date	
	Note	

No	Bank	
	Account Number	
	Password	
	Opening date	
	Note	

No	Bank	
	Account Number	
	Password	
	Opening date	
	Note	

No	PC	
	Account Number	
	Password	
	Opening date	
	Note	

No	Bank	
	Account Number	
	Password	
	Opening date	
	Note	

No	Bank	
	Account Number	
	Password	
	Opening date	
	Note	

No	PC	
	Account Number	
	Password	
	Opening date	
	Note	

No		
	Bank	
	Account Number	
	Password	
	Opening date	
	Note	

No		
	Bank	
	Account Number	
	Password	
	Opening date	
	Note	

No		
	PC	
	Account Number	
	Password	
	Opening date	
	Note	

No	Bank	
	Account Number	
	Password	
	Opening date	
	Note	

No	Bank	
	Account Number	
	Password	
	Opening date	
	Note	

No	PC	
	Account Number	
	Password	
	Opening date	
	Note	

No	Bank	
	Account Number	
	Password	
	Opening date	
	Note	

No	Bank	
	Account Number	
	Password	
	Opening date	
	Note	

No	PC	
	Account Number	
	Password	
	Opening date	
	Note	

No	Bank	
	Account Number	
	Password	
	Opening date	
	Note	

No	Bank	
	Account Number	
	Password	
	Opening date	
	Note	

No	PC	
	Account Number	
	Password	
	Opening date	
	Note	

No	Bank	
	Account Number	
	Password	
	Opening date	
	Note	

No	Bank	
	Account Number	
	Password	
	Opening date	
	Note	

No	PC	
	Account Number	
	Password	
	Opening date	
	Note	

No	Bank	
	Account Number	
	Password	
	Opening date	
	Note	

No	Bank	
	Account Number	
	Password	
	Opening date	
	Note	

No	PC	
	Account Number	
	Password	
	Opening date	
	Note	

No			
	Bank		
		Account Number	
		Password	
		Opening date	
		Note	

No			
	Bank		
		Account Number	
		Password	
		Opening date	
		Note	

No			
	PC		
		Account Number	
		Password	
		Opening date	
		Note	

No	Bank	
	Account Number	
	Password	
	Opening date	
	Note	

No	Bank	
	Account Number	
	Password	
	Opening date	
	Note	

No	PC	
	Account Number	
	Password	
	Opening date	
	Note	

No	Bank	
	Account Number	
	Password	
	Opening date	
	Note	

No	Bank	
	Account Number	
	Password	
	Opening date	
	Note	

No	PC	
	Account Number	
	Password	
	Opening date	
	Note	

No	Bank	
	Account Number	
	Password	
	Opening date	
	Note	

No	Bank	
	Account Number	
	Password	
	Opening date	
	Note	

No	PC	
	Account Number	
	Password	
	Opening date	
	Note	

No	Bank	
	Account Number	
	Password	
	Opening date	
	Note	

No	Bank	
	Account Number	
	Password	
	Opening date	
	Note	

No	PC	
	Account Number	
	Password	
	Opening date	
	Note	

No	Bank	
	Account Number	
	Password	
	Opening date	
	Note	

No	Bank	
	Account Number	
	Password	
	Opening date	
	Note	

No	PC	
	Account Number	
	Password	
	Opening date	
	Note	

No	Bank	
	Account Number	
	Password	
	Opening date	
	Note	

No	Bank	
	Account Number	
	Password	
	Opening date	
	Note	

No	PC	
	Account Number	
	Password	
	Opening date	
	Note	

No	Bank	
	Account Number	
	Password	
	Opening date	
	Note	

No	Bank	
	Account Number	
	Password	
	Opening date	
	Note	

No	PC	
	Account Number	
	Password	
	Opening date	
	Note	

No	Bank	
	Account Number	
	Password	
	Opening date	
	Note	

No	Bank	
	Account Number	
	Password	
	Opening date	
	Note	

No	PC	
	Account Number	
	Password	
	Opening date	
	Note	

No	Bank	
	Account Number	
	Password	
	Opening date	
	Note	

No	Bank	
	Account Number	
	Password	
	Opening date	
	Note	

No	PC	
	Account Number	
	Password	
	Opening date	
	Note	

No	Bank	
	Account Number	
	Password	
	Opening date	
	Note	

No	Bank	
	Account Number	
	Password	
	Opening date	
	Note	

No	PC	
	Account Number	
	Password	
	Opening date	
	Note	

No	Bank	
	Account Number	
	Password	
	Opening date	
	Note	

No	Bank	
	Account Number	
	Password	
	Opening date	
	Note	

No	PC	
	Account Number	
	Password	
	Opening date	
	Note	

No	Bank	
	Account Number	
	Password	
	Opening date	
	Note	

No	Bank	
	Account Number	
	Password	
	Opening date	
	Note	

No	PC	
	Account Number	
	Password	
	Opening date	
	Note	

No	Bank	
	Account Number	
	Password	
	Opening date	
	Note	

No	Bank	
	Account Number	
	Password	
	Opening date	
	Note	

No	PC	
	Account Number	
	Password	
	Opening date	
	Note	

No	Bank	
	Account Number	
	Password	
	Opening date	
	Note	

No	Bank	
	Account Number	
	Password	
	Opening date	
	Note	

No	PC	
	Account Number	
	Password	
	Opening date	
	Note	

No	Bank	
	Account Number	
	Password	
	Opening date	
	Note	

No	Bank	
	Account Number	
	Password	
	Opening date	
	Note	

No	PC	
	Account Number	
	Password	
	Opening date	
	Note	

No	Bank	
	Account Number	
	Password	
	Opening date	
	Note	

No	Bank	
	Account Number	
	Password	
	Opening date	
	Note	

No	PC	
	Account Number	
	Password	
	Opening date	
	Note	

No	Bank	
	Account Number	
	Password	
	Opening date	
	Note	

No	Bank	
	Account Number	
	Password	
	Opening date	
	Note	

No	PC	
	Account Number	
	Password	
	Opening date	
	Note	

No	Bank	
	Account Number	
	Password	
	Opening date	
	Note	

No	Bank	
	Account Number	
	Password	
	Opening date	
	Note	

No	PC	
	Account Number	
	Password	
	Opening date	
	Note	

No	Bank	
	Account Number	
	Password	
	Opening date	
	Note	

No	Bank	
	Account Number	
	Password	
	Opening date	
	Note	

No	PC	
	Account Number	
	Password	
	Opening date	
	Note	

No	Bank	
	Account Number	
	Password	
	Opening date	
	Note	

No	Bank	
	Account Number	
	Password	
	Opening date	
	Note	

No	PC	
	Account Number	
	Password	
	Opening date	
	Note	

No	Bank	
	Account Number	
	Password	
	Opening date	
	Note	

No	Bank	
	Account Number	
	Password	
	Opening date	
	Note	

No	PC	
	Account Number	
	Password	
	Opening date	
	Note	

No	Bank	
	Account Number	
	Password	
	Opening date	
	Note	

No	Bank	
	Account Number	
	Password	
	Opening date	
	Note	

No	PC	
	Account Number	
	Password	
	Opening date	
	Note	

No	Bank	
	Account Number	
	Password	
	Opening date	
	Note	

No	Bank	
	Account Number	
	Password	
	Opening date	
	Note	

No	PC	
	Account Number	
	Password	
	Opening date	
	Note	

No			
	Bank		
		Account Number	
		Password	
		Opening date	
		Note	

No			
	Bank		
		Account Number	
		Password	
		Opening date	
		Note	

No			
	PC		
		Account Number	
		Password	
		Opening date	
		Note	

No	**Bank**	
	Account Number	
	Password	
	Opening date	
	Note	

No	**Bank**	
	Account Number	
	Password	
	Opening date	
	Note	

No	**PC**	
	Account Number	
	Password	
	Opening date	
	Note	

No	Bank	
	Account Number	
	Password	
	Opening date	
	Note	

No	Bank	
	Account Number	
	Password	
	Opening date	
	Note	

No	PC	
	Account Number	
	Password	
	Opening date	
	Note	

No	Bank	
	Account Number	
	Password	
	Opening date	
	Note	

No	Bank	
	Account Number	
	Password	
	Opening date	
	Note	

No	PC	
	Account Number	
	Password	
	Opening date	
	Note	

No	Bank	
	Account Number	
	Password	
	Opening date	
	Note	

No	Bank	
	Account Number	
	Password	
	Opening date	
	Note	

No	PC	
	Account Number	
	Password	
	Opening date	
	Note	

No	Bank	
	Account Number	
	Password	
	Opening date	
	Note	

No	Bank	
	Account Number	
	Password	
	Opening date	
	Note	

No	PC	
	Account Number	
	Password	
	Opening date	
	Note	

No	Bank	
	Account Number	
	Password	
	Opening date	
	Note	

No	Bank	
	Account Number	
	Password	
	Opening date	
	Note	

No	PC	
	Account Number	
	Password	
	Opening date	
	Note	

No	Bank	
	Account Number	
	Password	
	Opening date	
	Note	

No	Bank	
	Account Number	
	Password	
	Opening date	
	Note	

No	PC	
	Account Number	
	Password	
	Opening date	
	Note	

No	Bank	
	Account Number	
	Password	
	Opening date	
	Note	

No	Bank	
	Account Number	
	Password	
	Opening date	
	Note	

No	PC	
	Account Number	
	Password	
	Opening date	
	Note	

No	Bank	
	Account Number	
	Password	
	Opening date	
	Note	

No	Bank	
	Account Number	
	Password	
	Opening date	
	Note	

No	PC	
	Account Number	
	Password	
	Opening date	
	Note	

No	Bank	
	Account Number	
	Password	
	Opening date	
	Note	

No	Bank	
	Account Number	
	Password	
	Opening date	
	Note	

No	PC	
	Account Number	
	Password	
	Opening date	
	Note	

No	Bank	
	Account Number	
	Password	
	Opening date	
	Note	

No	Bank	
	Account Number	
	Password	
	Opening date	
	Note	

No	PC	
	Account Number	
	Password	
	Opening date	
	Note	

www.ingramcontent.com/pod-product-compliance
Lightning Source LLC
Chambersburg PA
CBHW081741220526
45468CB00008B/2192